Planning for Learning through TOYS

Penny Coltman, Rachel Sparks Linfield and Lesley Hendy
Edited by Kate Element Illustrated by Cathy Hughes

Contents

Published by Step Forward Publishing Limited
Connaught House, Morrell Street, Leamington Spa, CV32 5SZ Tel: 01926 420042

Planning for Learning through Toys ISBN: 1-902438-00-0

MAKING PLANS

WHY PLAN?

The purpose of planning is to make sure that all children enjoy a broad and balanced curriculum. All planning should be useful. Plans are working documents which you spend time preparing, but which should later repay your efforts. Try to be concise. This will help you in finding information quickly when you need it.

LONG TERM PLANS

Preparing a long-term plan, which maps out the curriculum during a year or even two, will help you to ensure that you are providing a variety of activities and are meeting the statutory requirements of the Desirable Outcomes for Children's Learning on entering compulsory education (1997).

Your long-term plan need not be detailed. Divide the time period over which you are planning into fairly equal sections, such as half terms. Choose a topic for each section as young children benefit from making links between the new ideas they encounter. As you select each topic, think about the time of year in which you plan to do it. A topic about minibeasts will not be very successful in November!

Although each topic will address all the learning areas, some could focus on a specific area. For example, a topic on Spring would lend itself well to activities relating to knowledge and understanding of the living world. Another topic might particularly encourage the appreciation of stories. Try to make sure that you provide a variety of topics in your long-term plans.

Autumn 1	Me and my family
Autumn 2	Christmas
Spring 1	Once upon a time
Spring 2	Spring
Summer 1	Toys
Summer 2	Out and about

MEDIUM TERM PLANS

Medium term plans will outline the contents of a topic in a little more detail. One way to start this process is by brainstorming on a large piece of paper. Work with your team writing down all the activities you can think of which are relevant to the topic. As you do this it may become clear that some activities go well together. Think about dividing them into themes, the topic of toys for example has themes such as moving toys, puppets, teddy bears' picnic.

At this stage it is helpful to make a chart. Write the theme ideas down the side of the chart and put a different area of learning at the top of each column. Now you can insert your brainstormed ideas and will quickly see where there are gaps. As you complete the chart take account of children's earlier experiences and provide opportunities for them to progress.

Refer back to the Desirable Outcomes document and check that you have addressed as many different aspects of it as you can. Once all your medium-term plans are complete make sure that there are no neglected areas.

DAY TO DAY PLANS

The plans you make for each day will outline aspects such as:

- resources needed;
- the way in which you might introduce activities;
- the organisation of adult help;
- size of the group;
- timing.

Identify the learning which each activity is intended to promote. Make a note of any assessments or observations which you are likely to carry out. On your plans make notes of which activities were particularly successful, or any changes you would make another time.

MAKING PLANS

A FINAL NOTE

Planning should be seen as flexible. Not all groups meet every day, and not all children attend every day. Any part of the plans in this book can be used independently, stretched over a longer period or condensed to meet the needs of any group. You will almost certainly adapt the activities as children respond to them in different ways and bring their own ideas, interests and enthusiasms. Be prepared to be flexible over timing as some ideas prove more popular than others. The important thing is to ensure that the children are provided with a varied and enjoyable curriculum which meets their individual developing needs.

USING THE BOOK

- Collect or prepare suggested resources as listed on page 21.
- Read the section which outlines links to the Desirable Outcomes document (pages 4 - 7) and explains the rationale for the topic of Toys.
- For each weekly theme two activities are described in detail as examples to help you in your planning and preparation. Key vocabulary, questions and learning opportunities are identified.
- The skills chart on pages 22 - 23 will help you to see at a glance which aspects of children's development are being addressed as a focus each week.
- As children take part in the toy topic activities, their learning will progress. Collecting evidence on page 3 explains how you might monitor children's achievements.
- Find out on page 20 how the topic can be brought together in a grand finale involving parents, children and friends.
- There is additional material to support the working partnership of families and children in the form of a home links page, and a photocopiable parent's page found at the back of the book.

It is important to appreciate that the ideas presented in this book will only be a part of your planning. Many activities which will be taking place as routine in your group may not be mentioned. For example, it is assumed that sand, dough, water, puzzles, floor toys and large scale apparatus are part of the ongoing pre-school experience. Role play areas, stories, rhymes and singing, and group discussion times are similarly assumed to be happening in each week although they may not be a focus for described activities.

USING THE DESIRABLE OUTCOMES FOR CHILDREN'S LEARNING

Having decided on your topic and made your medium term plans you can use the document produced by the Department of Education and Employment called *Desirable Outcomes for Children's Learning on entering compulsory education* to highlight the key learning opportunities your activities will address. The desirable outcomes are split into six areas: Personal and Social Development, Language and Literacy, Mathematics, Knowledge and Understanding of the World, Physical Development and Creative Development. Do not expect each of your topics to cover every outcome but your long-term plans should allow for all the outcomes to be addressed.

The following section highlights parts of the desirable outcomes document in point form to show what children are expected to be able to do by the time they enter compulsory education in each area of learning. These points will be used throughout this book to show how activities for a topic on toys link to these expectations. For example, Personal and Social Development point 2 is 'work as part of a group and independently'. Activities suggested which provide the opportunity for children to do this will have the reference PS2. This will enable you to see which parts of the desirable outcomes are covered in a given week and plan for areas to be revisited and developed.

In addition you can ensure that activities offer variety in the outcomes to be encountered. Often a similar activity may be carried out to achieve different learning outcomes. For example, children can make puppets for a variety of reasons. On page 15 an activity to make paper plate puppets is described. It aims to encourage children to focus on facial features and to look for similarities and differences between humans in order to meet outcomes within Knowledge and Understanding of the World. At the same time, children will also be using a variety of skills which feature in the Physical Development outcomes and also a range of tools and materials which are covered by Creative Development. It is important therefore that activities have clearly defined learning outcomes so that these may be emphasised during the activity and for recording purposes.

PERSONAL AND SOCIAL DEVELOPMENT (PS)

These outcomes consider important aspects of development which affect the ways children learn, behave and relate to others.

Children will:

- PS1 be confident, show appropriate self-respect and establish effective relationships with other children and with adults
- PS2 work as part of a group and independently
- PS3 concentrate and persevere in their learning and seek help where needed
- PS4 be eager to explore new learning and show ability to initiate ideas and solve simple problems
- PS5 demonstrate independence in selecting an activity or resources and in dressing and personal hygiene
- PS6 be sensitive to the needs and feelings of others and show respect for people of other cultures and beliefs
- PS7 take turns and share fairly

PS8 express their feelings and behave in appropriate ways developing an understanding of what is right, what is wrong and why

PS9 treat living things properly and their environment with care and concern

PS10 respond to relevant cultural and religious events and show a range of feelings such as wonder, joy or sorrow, in response to their experiences of the world

On a general level children can learn to share and take turns by playing with toys (PS7) but specific activities on toys throughout the weekly themes encourage particular parts of Personal and Social Development. Inevitably many outcomes will also develop as a natural result of activities in other key areas. For example, when children collaborate to build towers from toy bricks to develop Knowledge and Understanding of the World they will also have the opportunity to further PS2, 3 and 4.

LANGUAGE AND LITERACY (L)

The Language and Literacy outcomes provide the basis for developing children's ability to read and write with enthusiasm, interest and confidence.

Children will:

L1 use a growing vocabulary with increasing fluency to express thoughts and convey meaning to the listener

L2 listen and respond to stories, songs, nursery rhymes and poems

L3 participate in role-play with confidence

L4 enjoy books and handle them carefully

L5 understand how books are organised

L6 know that words and pictures carry meaning

L7 begin to associate sounds and patterns in rhymes, with syllables and with written words and letters

L8 recognise their own names and some familiar words

L9 recognise letters of the alphabet by shape and sound

L10 use pictures, symbols, familiar words and letters to communicate meaning

L11 develop an awareness of some of the purposes of writing

L12 write their names with appropriate use of upper and lower case letters

The activities suggested for the theme of puppets provide the opportunity for children to respond to a variety of imaginative situations including responding to stories and participating in role-play. The writing of labels for displays and picture menus for a teddy bears' picnic will help children to develop their early writing skills which may start with picture labels and progress to beginning to form letters. The use of labels will help children to know that words and pictures carry meaning and therefore gives purpose to their own writing. Throughout all the activities children will be encouraged to communicate fluently and with meaning.

MATHEMATICS (M)

These outcomes cover important aspects of mathematical understanding and provide the foundation for numeracy. They focus on achievement through practical activities and on using and understanding language in the development of simple mathematical ideas.

Children will:

- M1 use mathematical language, such as circle, in front of, bigger than and more, to describe shape, position, size and quantity
- M2 recognise and recreate patterns
- M3 be familiar with number rhymes, songs, stories, counting games and activities
- M4 compare, sort, match, order, sequence and count using everyday objects
- M5 recognise and use numbers to 10 and are familiar with larger numbers from their everyday lives
- M6 begin to use their developing mathematical understanding to solve practical problems
- M7 through practical activities understand and record numbers, begin to show awareness of number operations, such as addition and subtraction, and begin to use the language involved

Toys are a natural focus for children's attention and this will encourage them to join in conversation, using a range of descriptive mathematical vocabulary (M1). Several games are suggested in which children jump, clap or skip, etc, a given number of times which will reinforce number skills (M3 & 5). Specific activities concentrate on individual numbers, helping children to develop mental images of these numbers ie when they see three toy soldiers in a row they know there are three without going through the process of counting, one, two, three. These activities will consolidate their understandings of number (M5). Toys are also particularly good objects to sort, compare and order. As children sort toys into sets, or rank a line of teddies in order of size, they will build a working vocabulary of descriptive and comparative language (M4), for example the teddy with the red bow is bigger than the teddy with the blue jumper.

Finally, the teddy bears' picnic which forms the grand finale of the topic, places all the mathematics of the term within a practical, meaningful and very 'real' context (M6).

KNOWLEDGE AND UNDERSTANDING OF THE WORLD (K)

Children will:

- K1 talk about where they live, their environment, their families and past and present events in their own lives
- K2 explore and recognise features of living things, objects and events in the natural and made world
- K3 look closely at similarities, differences, patterns and change
- K4 show awareness of the purposes of some features of the area in which they live

K5 talk about observations, recording them sometimes

K6 ask questions to gain information about why things happen and how things work

K7 explore and select materials and equipment

K8 use skills such as cutting, joining, folding and building for a variety of purposes

K9 use technology where appropriate to support learning

The topic of toys provides an opportunity to help children experience K3, 5, 6, 7 and 8. In addition they will begin to touch on K1, 2 and 4. For example, when talking about old toys children can be encouraged to discuss their favourite toys from when they were babies. In this way children will begin to talk about past events in their lives. Similarly, when working with construction toys children may make layouts of towns and villages. Discussion of why particular features have been included could result in children showing an awareness of K4.

PHYSICAL DEVELOPMENT (PD)

These outcomes explore a wide range of fine and gross motor skills which are useful throughout all areas of life.

Children will:

PD1 move confidently and imaginatively with increasing control and co-ordination and an awareness of space and others

PD2 use a range of small and large equipment and balancing and climbing apparatus, with increasing skill

PD3 handle appropriate tools, objects, construction and malleable materials safely and with increasing control

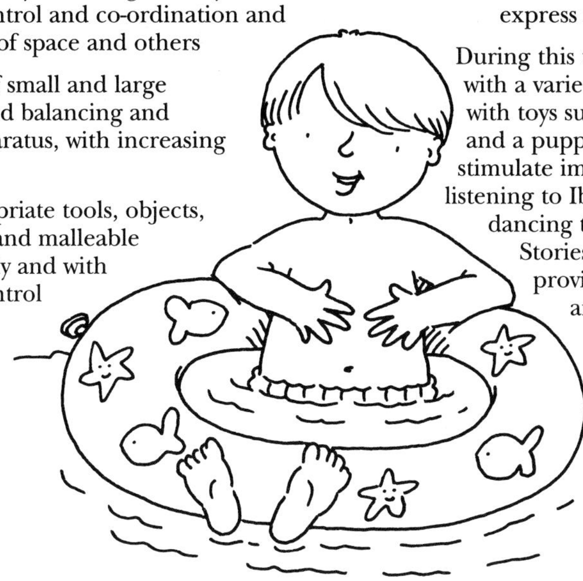

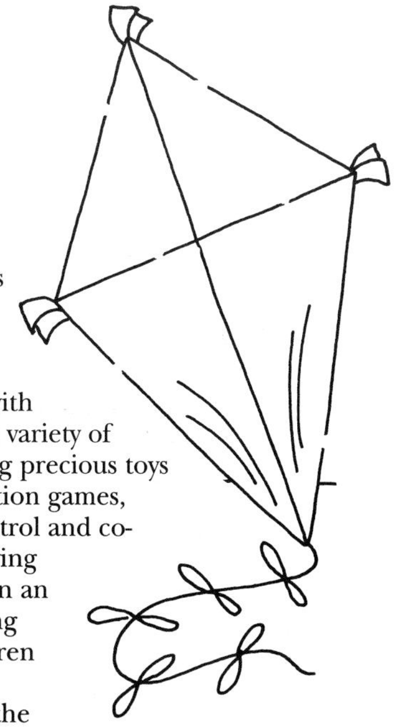

Activities such as making puppets, jack-in-the-boxes and items for the teddy bears' picnic will offer suitable experiences of PD3. Through building with construction toys, using a variety of types of puppets, handling precious toys sensitively and playing action games, children can develop control and co-ordination whilst also having the opportunity to work in an imaginative way. By playing whole group games children will become aware of the restrictions of space and the needs of others.

CREATIVE DEVELOPMENT (C)

Children will:

C1 explore sound and colour, texture, shape, form and space in two and three dimensions

C2 respond in a variety of ways to what they see, hear, smell, touch and feel

C3 through art, music and dance, stories and imaginative play show an increasing ability to use their imagination, to listen and to observe

C4 use a widening range of materials, suitable tools, instruments and other resources to express ideas and to communicate their feelings

During this topic children will experience working with a variety of materials as they make and play with toys such as making different types of puppets and a puppet theatre. Music and dance are used to stimulate imaginative responses, for example listening to Ibert's *Fantastic Toy Shop* and then dancing to it in the 'Favourite toys' theme. Stories and games throughout the topic provide a key stimulus for listening, looking and responding.

Week 1

FAVOURITE TOYS

PERSONAL AND SOCIAL DEVELOPMENT

- Encourage children to handle others' toys with sensitivity and care. (PS6)
- Discuss ways favourite toys can be looked after. (PS6)
- Encourage children to share favourite toys and play collaboratively. (PS7)

LANGUAGE AND LITERACY

- Ask children to talk about their favourite toy. (L1)
- Ask each child their toy's name and make a name label. At this stage you need to explain the reason for labels - to know the name of everyone else's toy - to help them understand the need for writing. Depending on their ability, some children will watch you write, others will attempt to make their own labels. Display the toys with their labels. (L8, 10)
- Hide some favourite toys in a bag and ask children to feel and describe a toy. Can other children identify the toy from the description? (L1)

MATHEMATICS

- Use bubble blowing (everybody's favourite!) to promote language describing shape, size, number and movement. (M1)
- Use hoop games to establish words 'round', 'circle', 'roll'. (M1)
- Reinforce using a collection of favourite toys which are round - balls, wheels of tractors, cars, bicycles. Do some printing with round shapes. (M1)

KNOWLEDGE AND UNDERSTANDING OF THE WORLD

- Explore children's favourite nursery school toys. Compare children's choices. Play with them! (K2)
- Extend the bubble-blowing by using a variety of blowers, straws, funnels, hoops to make large bubbles. You will need a large bowl with washing-up liquid bubble solution. (K6, 7)
- Sort favourite toys into categories such as construction toys, outside toys, moving toys. (K3)

PHYSICAL DEVELOPMENT

- Roll hoops. (PD2)
- Take your toy for a walk along a prepared track of bean bags or cones and talk about direction and position. (PD1)

CREATIVE DEVELOPMENT

- Use powder paints to make paintings of favourite toys. (C1)
- Listen to music about toys (Ibert's *Fantastic Toy Shop*; Leopold Mozart's *The Toy Symphony*; Tchaikovsky's *Nutcracker Suite*). Dance to the music. (C2, 3)
- Set up a toy shop in the role play corner. (C3)

ACTIVITY: Telling the story of a favourite toy

Learning opportunity: Children will develop an awareness of the ways in which some possessions are precious.

Desirable Learning Outcome: Personal and Social Development. Children are sensitive to the needs and feelings of others.

Resources: A favourite toy per child, a toy which is special to the leading adult.

Organisation: Small group or whole group.

WHAT TO DO:

- Bring a favourite toy of your own to the group.
- Show it to the children and explain exactly why it is so special. Does the toy have a name? What does it feel like to touch? Does it have any special features?
- Talk about how you came by the toy. Was it given as a gift from a special person?
- Tell stories about any adventures you may have had with the toy, perhaps a day it was lost and then found. How did you feel?
- Talk about how the toy has been a special friend. Did you talk to it when you were unhappy or share exciting news?
- Encourage the children to tell each other about their favourite toys. How are they special?

ACTIVITY: Blowing bubbles

Learning opportunity: Children will observe and describe bubbles. They will select equipment to make large bubbles.

Desirable Learning Outcome: Knowledge and Understanding of the World. Children will look closely at differences and similarities, and change. They will talk about their observations, explore and select equipment.

Resources: Selection of bubble blowers, such as funnels attached to rubber tubing, two straws with thick cotton through them, wire coat hanger with hook bent and taped so that it is safe, yoghurt pots of a variety of sizes with holes (approx 1 x 2 cm) in the bottom, bubble solution (half a cup of baby bubble bath, 1 cup of Gelozone - can be bought in health shops, 2 cups of water, quarter cup of glycerine), small quantity of cheap, ready-made bubble solution, washing up bowl per pair of children, waterproof aprons.

Organisation: Small group either outside or in an area suitable for wet activity.

Key vocabulary: Bubble, round, slippery, wet, solution, float.

WHAT TO DO:

Blow a bubble using the cheap, ready-made solution. (Bubbles from this are usually quite small and will not last long.) Ask the children to describe what they see. Consider the sizes, colours, time before bursting and the way they travel. Could bubbles be made without blowing? Demonstrate waving the blower. What is the difference between that and blowing? Show the children the washing up bowls with the made-up solution and the variety of blowers. Challenge the children to make the largest bubble they can. Ask them which equipment they think will work best. Why?

NB Where equipment is likely to touch children's mouths (eg yoghurt pot blowers) ensure that there is one per child and that children do not use each others' blowers. The straw and cotton frames can be used to collect a film of bubble solution. If raised slowly above the head, huge bubbles can result. It takes time and practice to do this but a demonstration usually enthuses the children to try. It can also be excellent for hand co-ordination skills.

DISPLAY

Make a table display of favourite toys of the group. Children should be asked which ones they would like to put on the display and why. Care should be taken not to overload the table. It should provide an introduction to the toys topic. Each day before the children arrive one toy could be replaced by another. Children will enjoy spotting which toy has been taken away and what has replaced it. Paintings of favourite toys can be displayed on a nearby board or made into a book of favourite toys. Children should be encouraged to show their parents around the display in order to share their learning and also to stimulate further interest in the topic. This sharing should be encouraged for all displays in future weeks.

Week 2

CONSTRUCTION TOYS

PERSONAL AND SOCIAL DEVELOPMENT

- Encourage children to solve problems such as building a tower that is as high as a chair seat. (PS4)
- Discuss the importance of taking turns and sharing when constructing. (PS7, 8)

LANGUAGE AND LITERACY

- In small groups discuss ways of constructing something. What shall we build? What do we need? (L1)
- Write name labels to show who made a model, highlighting the reason for the label. Encourage older children to write their own name label, younger children may draw a picture of themselves as a label. (L8, 12)
- Use a names rota for using different toys. Encourage the children to recognise their own names and, gradually, the names of their friends. (L8)

MATHEMATICS

- Use stacking toys to introduce and reinforce comparative vocabulary, smallest, smaller, bigger, biggest. (M4)
- Order towers by height, roads and bridges by length. (M4)

KNOWLEDGE AND UNDERSTANDING OF THE WORLD

- Build brick towers. How tall are they before they fall? (K2, 5)
- Make houses from different types of construction toys. (K4, 7)
- Compare brick patterns with real homes. Make wax crayon rubbings of brick patterns. (K3, 4)

PHYSICAL DEVELOPMENT

- Mime being builders. (PD1)
- Set challenges which require fine motor co-ordination such as tower building or balancing bricks. (PD3)
- Balance on different body parts. (PD1)

CREATIVE DEVELOPMENT

- Build models using 3-D materials, for example build a track for a puppet to walk along. (C4)
- Make up a dance about moving like machines. Suitable music will be found on BBC sound effects tapes or try *I like Driving in my Car* by Madness (listen for the sound effects at the start) and *Money* by Pink Floyd. (C3)

ACTIVITY: Building toy houses based on *Miss Brick the Builder's Baby*

Learning opportunity: Children will listen to the story of *Miss Brick the Builder's Baby* by Allan Ahlberg and Colin McNaughton (Puffin Books) and use it as a focus for role play.

Desirable Learning Outcome: Language and Literacy: Children will listen and respond to a story, take part in role play and enjoy books.

Resources: *Miss Brick the Builder's Baby*; brightly coloured building bricks.

Organisation: Whole group.

Key vocabulary: Builder, built, build.

WHAT TO DO:

Read the story to the group. Discuss the pictures of buildings and in particular the ones where Mr and Mrs Brick get things wrong with the building of their houses. Encourage children to join in with phrases which are repeated such as '"Our baby does not build!" said Mr Brick. "She knocks things down!" Mrs Brick said'. Talk about things the children like to build. Which are their favourite construction toys? Ask children to look at the pictures of the houses Baby Brick built for the new Baby Brick. Suggest they work in pairs or threes to build similar houses. Encourage the children to look at the colours and shapes. Some children may like to take on the role of a member of the Brick family. Later in the week discuss what might happen next in the story.

ACTIVITY: Using stacking toys

Learning opportunity: Children will develop comparative language as they explore the use of stacking toys.

Desirable Learning Outcome: Mathematics. Children use mathematical language. They compare, sort, match, order, sequence and count using everyday objects.

Resources: A selection of stacking toys: bricks, pots or boxes.

Organisation: Small group.

Key vocabulary: Small, smaller, smallest, tall, taller, tallest, height, more, less.

WHAT TO DO:

- As the children play with stacking toys offer a series of challenges.
- Can you make more than one tower? Which is the tallest? Which is the smallest?
- Can you put your towers in order? Put the tallest one at this end. Put the smallest one at this end.
- How could you make this tower taller?
- How could you make this tower less tall?
- Can you put some more bricks on this tower? How has the height changed, is it taller or smaller?
- Take some bricks off this one. How has the height changed now?

DISPLAY

Start the week with a clear table covered by a grassy coloured material or paper. Models made during the week can be placed by the children on the display with their own labels. Children should be encouraged to think about the overall effect and to realise that their model does not have to be at the front or in the centre!

Week 3

MOVING TOYS

PERSONAL AND SOCIAL DEVELOPMENT

- Provide opportunities for exploring the moving toys through sharing. (PS7)
- Discuss how it feels to move in different ways. (PS8)

LANGUAGE AND LITERACY

- To develop positional language ask small groups of children to make their toys move under, behind, through, over boxes. Ask them to describe how their friends are moving toys. (L1,6)
- Sit the children in a circle around a box obstacle course for a moving toy. Invite each child to say an action word and you move the toy accordingly. (L1)
- On large sheets of paper using thick crayons ask children to take a line for a walk talking about going up, down and so on. (L1)

MATHEMATICS

- Compare the distances travelled by wheeled vehicles. (M4)
- Spot the shapes on moving toys: round wheels, square doors, oblong windows. (M1)
- Roll old toy cars over a paint sponge and print the tracks. Talk about shapes and patterns. (M1)

KNOWLEDGE AND UNDERSTANDING OF THE WORLD

- Observe moving toys such as tops, yo-yos. Compare how they move. What starts them? What stops them? (K5, 6)
- Make some jack-in-a-box using card folded as a concertina for the spring mechanism. (K8)
- Play with cars down ramps of varying heights. How far do the cars travel before stopping? (K5, 6)
- Make and observe paper windmills. Compare with bought versions. (K5, 8)

PHYSICAL DEVELOPMENT

- Be a jack-in-the-box. (PD1)
- Let's be trains! (PD1)

CREATIVE DEVELOPMENT

- Make simple finger puppets by cutting out pictures and sticking them to paper 'rings'. (C4)
- Make up dances for jumping jacks, dancing dolls etc. (C3)

ACTIVITY: Making a jack-in-the-box

Learning opportunity: Through observing a jack-in-the-box children will learn about the action of springs. They will cut and fold card to make a spring.

Desirable Learning Outcome: Knowledge and Understanding of the World. Children will ask questions to gain information about how things work and use skills such as cutting and folding.

Resources: A real jack-in-the-box; a pair of card strips (approx 4 x 30 cm) stapled at right angles for each child; scissors; staplers; felt pens/crayons.

Organisation: Whole group introduction, six children per adult for the practical work.

Key vocabulary: Spring, push, up, down.

WHAT TO DO:

Show the children a jack-in-the-box closed. How heavy is it? Does it rattle? What do they think is in the box? Open the box, what happened? Why do they think that the jack-in-the-box has popped up? Let the children carefully close the box and experience the force of the spring pushing up. Encourage them to describe what they feel. Explain that they are going to make jacks on cardboard springs. Demonstrate how two strips of card can be folded to make a spring. Work with the children. Compress the spring on a table and release it. What happens? Draw and colour a Jack on cardboard, then cut it out with a tab to staple it to the spring. Allow the children time to play with them. Then try sticking the springs into a small box to make a jack-in-the-box. Explore what happens if you use longer strips of card.

ACTIVITY: Let's be trains!

Learning opportunity: Children will work collaboratively, moving together within a role play context.

Desirable Learning Outcome: Physical development. Children will move confidently and imaginatively with an awareness of space and others.

Resources: Playground chalk, whistle.

Organisation: Whole group.

Key vocabulary: Stop, start, getting slower, getting faster, turn, wait.

WHAT TO DO:

Prepare this activity by drawing a series of lines on the floor or outside ground, to represent train tracks. If you are lucky enough to have access to a school playground which is marked out for netball, these lines are ideal.

Introduce the activity by discussing favourite stories about trains. Explain to the children that they are going to pretend to be trains. Depending on the size of the group, choose two or three children to be engines, but explain that others will get a turn. Allocate a small group of children to each 'engine' showing them how to hold on to each other so that their train does not fall apart. Show them how they are going to move along the tracks and talk about the importance of staying on them. Most importantly, explain that when the trains hear the station master's whistle they must stop immediately. This allows you to use the whistle for prevention of accidents as well as for signalling new instructions.

There are several important roles for the remaining children: passengers, signals (who must warn if the trains are likely to collide), engineers (who must rush to the scene if a trains break down), children to join hands above the track to make a tunnel, and so on.

Now put yourself in role as the 'station master' and have fun directing the running of the trains.

NB Children find moving whilst holding onto each other quite difficult. It is important to keep the speed of the 'engines' down to prevent those following behind from falling.

DISPLAY

Any models of buildings from Week 2 can be kept to form the basis for a town/street for children to play with toy cars. A second table is useful for providing a collection of safe, wooden moving toys such as teddies which fall down ladders, a Jacob's ladder, acrobat, jack-in-the-box. A home-made jack-in-the-box made from card will stimulate interest for one of the week's activities.

Week 4

Puppets

Language and Literacy

- Make a collection of different kinds of puppets. Talk about what they can do. Play with them. (L1, 3)
- Read a simple version of the story of Pinnochio. (L2)
- Make a collection of action words which begin with the letter 'p' eg push, pull, paint, play. Which actions can the puppets perform?
- Make up a simple dialogue between two puppets. (L3)

Personal and Social Development

- Discuss with children how they could stage their puppet plays so that others can share their stories. (PS6)
- Use a puppet theatre to tell stories about people's feelings. (PS2, 6)
- Discuss appropriate behaviour for working in the puppet theatre. (PS8)
- Use the story of Pinnochio to discuss the importance of telling the truth. (PS8)

Mathematics

- Use finger puppets to illustrate number 'finger' rhymes such as Two Little Dicky Birds, Five Little Men in a Flying Saucer, Five Little Speckled Frogs. (M3).
- Use puppets to illustrate numbers 1-5. The puppet has 2 hands, 2 eyes, 1 nose, 3 buttons and so on. (M5).
- Number the parts of a simple puppet picture outline using numbers 1-6. Allocate each number a colour. Roll a dice to determine which areas can be coloured in (M5).
- Make finger puppets based on different 2D geometric shapes such as Trevor Triangle, Ozzie Oblong and use them as the basis for stories. Encourage the children to draw pictures using the 2D shapes made familiar by the puppets. Sticky geometric shapes could be used to help (M1).

Knowledge and Understanding of the World

- Use animal glove puppets to tell an animal story from around the world. Talk about the animals involved. (K2)
- Make puppets from cardboard plates attached to cardboard tubes. Encourage close observation of facial features. (K5, 7, 8)
- Observe a string puppet moving. How does it move? Which string is pulled to move the head? How can we make it walk? (K5, 6)

Physical Development

- Following instructions from an adult 'puppeteer' children move like string puppets (PD1)
- Sing 'Here we go round Pinnochio' to the tune of 'Mulberry Bush' including appropriate instructions. Before singing the song children should be encourage to look at a string puppet doing each of the actions so that they can copy the puppet and move in similar ways, only bending where the puppet bends. Children can be invited to suggest more verses such as 'This is the way we nod our head; tap a foot; clap our hands'.(PD1, 2)
- Give verbal instructions for children's puppets to follow. (PD2, 3)

Creative Development

- Build and decorate a puppet theatre from cardboard boxes. (C4)
- Make sound effects for puppet plays. (C2)
- Practise speaking in different voices for the puppets. (C2, 3)

ACTIVITY: Plate people puppets

Learning opportunity: Children will recognise features of living things. They will explore and select materials.

Desirable Learning Outcome: Knowledge and Understanding of the World. Children will observe features of faces and use this knowledge to make realistic people puppets from paper plates and scrap materials.

Resources: Paper plates; dowelling or cardboard tubes; crepe paper; scraps of wool; paper and fabric for making faces; glue; tape; scissors.

Organisation: Whole group introduction then groups of up to eight children to each adult helper for making the puppets.

Key vocabulary: Eyes, cheeks, nose, mouth, chin, ears.

WHAT TO DO:

Introduce the activity by talking about faces. Ask children to point to their eyes, cheeks, nose, mouth, chin and ears. Talk about hair colours and styles. Use mirrors to encourage children to look at their own faces. Explain that they are going to make people puppets.

Give each child a paper plate. Explain that the plate will become the head of a puppet. Ask children to think about who their puppet will be. Using wool, shredded paper, pens and so on the children can create their puppet.

Talk to individual children about their puppet. Is it a boy or a girl? Is it happy or sad? When finished, tape the plate onto a long cardboard tube or piece of doweling. Pleat a piece of crepe paper around the tube/stick for simple clothing. Encourage pairs of children to use their puppets to have conversations.

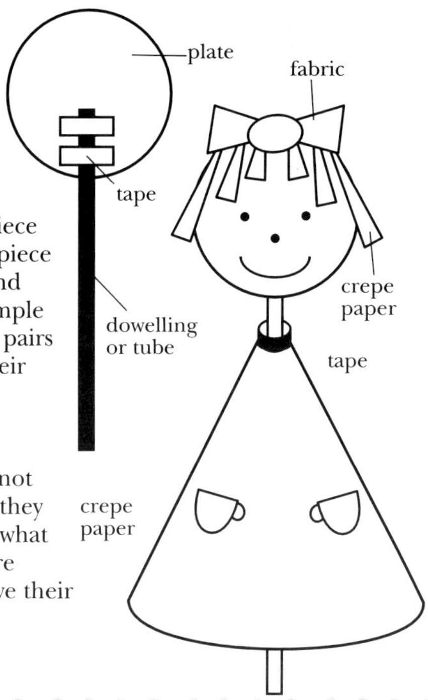

NB If children have not used mirrors before they will need to explore what mirrors can do before using them to observe their faces.

ACTIVITY: A puppet show

Learning opportunity: Children will develop the skills of speaking as they play with the puppets.

Desirable Learning Outcome: Language and Literacy. They use a growing vocabulary with increasing fluency to express thoughts and convey meaning to the listener.

Resources: Finger or glove puppets. Cardboard box puppet theatre or a table laid on its side to form a simple stage.

Organisation: Small group.

Key vocabulary: A range of everyday speech.

WHAT TO DO:

Talk to the children about the variety of puppets with which they are playing. What sort of characters do the children think the puppets are? Are they friendly, happy, sad or grumpy?

Encourage the children to think about the sorts of things which the puppets might say to demonstrate their characters. What sort of voices do they have?

What will the puppets say when they meet each other? What do we say?

What will the puppets say to the audience? How might they make the audience laugh?

How will the puppets talk about their adventures? Encourage some descriptive language which tells the audience what is happening.

How will the puppets say goodbye?

DISPLAY

Make a pretend puppet theatre out of a cardboard box turned on its side. Cut large holes in each side. In front of the box place a selection of old greetings cards featuring animals, characters and so on, some selotape and drinking straws. Show children how to make simple puppets by sticking cut-out pictures onto straws. Shows can be performed by manipulating the puppets through the sides of the box.

Week 5

Special toys

Personal and social development

- Talk about caring for toys that are old and precious. (PS8, 9)
- Encourage children to talk about how their own special toys are important to them. (PS6)
- Compare and contrast toys from different countries and talk about customs in those countries. (PS10)

Language and literacy

- Use an old toy to encourage language that describes the past for example, yesterday, a long time ago, when I was little. (L1)
- Look at old photographs or pictures of children playing with toys. Try to find some depicting old-fashioned hoops. Discuss what games the children might be playing. Do children play them now? (L1, 4)
- With a small group play an old game. Encourage the children to teach others the game. (L1)
- Look at a variety of toys from around the world such as Russian dolls which stack inside each other, American football, kites (China), boomerangs (Australia), dolls in national costume, origami animals (Japan), carved wooden animal (Africa). Discuss where they have come from. (L1)
- Show children where the toys come from on a globe. Display some pictures of the toys with labels of the countries of origin. (L8)

Mathematics

- Play target hoops - see activity on opposite page (M1, 3, 5)
- Use clockwork toys to introduce words which describe speed and distance. (M1)
- Use Russian dolls to revisit ordering by size, height. Use comparative vocabulary: bigger than, smaller than and so on; and positions: inside, outside, next to, between. (M1, 4)
- Make sets of given numbers of matching toys, using numbers 1-5 eg 3 toy soldiers, 3 dressed dolls. Children record by drawing. (M5)
- Make a collaborative display using pictures drawn and cut out by children. Arrange the 'toys' in sets and display the number in each set (M5).

Knowledge and understanding of the world

- Make a collection of moving wooden toys eg ball and cup, acrobat. Play with the toys. Ask children to describe how they move. (K5, 6)
- Look at an old doll and a modern one. Compare the materials from which they are made and their clothes. (K3)
- Make a collection of national costume dolls. Discuss where they have come from. Ask children to bring in photos of any countries they have visited. Match them to the dolls. (K1)

Physical development

- Play ring games: Farmer's in the den, Ring-a-ring of roses, Hokey cokey and so on. (PD1)
- March like toy soldiers. (PD1)
- Make large picture cards of large, medium and small Russian dolls. Encourage children to match the size of their actions - hop, jump, clap, step, skip - to the size of the doll. (PD1)

Creative development

- Use coloured chalks to make drawings of old toys through close observation. (Finished pictures can be taken outside by an adult and sprayed with hair spray to stop them smudging.) (C2, 4)
- Role play old toys telling stories of their pasts. (C3)
- Encourage children to dress up in the role play area in costumes from around the world. Who are they? Where do they live? What do they do? (C2, 3)

ACTIVITY: Target hoops

Learning opportunity: Children will recognise and describe a range of mathematical representations.

Desirable Learning Outcome: Mathematics. Children will recognise and use numbers to ten and will use mathematical language.

Resources: Prepared cards (see below).

Organisation: Small groups.

Key vocabulary: Numbers to five or ten. Shapes: square, circle, triangle. Comparative language: biggest, smallest, longest, shortest. Colour names.

WHAT TO DO:

This game can be easily adapted to include different aspects of mathematics, and to meet the needs of children of varying abilities. The basic principle is that four or five large hoops are laid on the ground. In each hoop is a card. In turn the children either aim a bean bag into a hoop nominated by an adult, or throw their bean bag and describe the card which is in the hoop in which it happens to land .

On the cards you might choose to draw various sets of objects ('Can you aim at the hoop with three bananas?'), numerals ('Can you aim at the hoop with the number 5?')or number words ('Which hoop has the word six in it?').

To encourage children to compare and describe different shapes use pictures of similar objects of different sizes - 'Throw your bean bag at the hoop with the biggest apples in it' - or similar objects of different colours - 'Which are the orange butterflies?'

Older and more able children will enjoy recognising and describing simple geometric shapes: 'My bean bag is in the hoop with the red triangle', 'Mine is in the one with the smallest square'.

ACTIVITY: The Russian doll game

Learning opportunity: Through playing the Russian doll game children will be encouraged to move in a variety of imaginative ways with particular emphasis on making their movements big, medium or small.

Desirable Learning Outcome: Physical development. Children will move confidently and imaginatively with increasing control, co-ordination and an awareness of space and others.

Resources: Large cut-outs of big, medium and small Russian dolls, real wooden Russian dolls.

Organisation: Whole group in a space large enough to allow for free movement.

Key vocabulary: Big, medium, small.

WHAT TO DO:

Show the group the real dolls. Show how they come apart and ask them to place them in order of height, starting with the tallest. Which is the biggest doll? Which is the smallest? Does anyone know a word to describe the other doll? Introduce the word medium if the children do not offer it.

Show the card dolls. Ask which is the medium-sized doll. Ask a child to jump. Ask if anyone can do a bigger jump. Can anyone show a smaller jump? Introduce the dolls as signs of the size of things they are going to do and ask the children to find a space. Hold up the small doll and ask them to do a jump. Praise those doing small jumps. Show another sized doll. Continue with actions such as striding, hopping, stretching. Bring the group together and ask someone to hop like one of the dolls. Can the others guess which doll has been chosen?

The game can be extended during the topic to use more doll cards and doing a sequence of actions such as two large jumps, one medium one and three small jumps. Encourage the children to move with control and imagination.

DISPLAY

Make a display of dolls wearing national costumes. In Week 4 alert parents to the theme for Week 5 and invite them to send in dolls and photographs or pictures of the countries from which the dolls have come.

Look back at the original 'Favourite toys' display with children. Are these toys still their favourites?

Week 6

TEDDY BEARS' PICNIC

PERSONAL AND SOCIAL DEVELOPMENT

- Talk about the need to wash hands and keep clean when preparing food. (PS5)
- Discuss appropriate behaviour for picnics and eating together. (PS8)
- Share the jobs for the picnic preparation and clearing away. (PS2, 7)

LANGUAGE AND LITERACY

- Make charts to show all the foods which teddy bears like. (L10)
- Make picture menus to list the different real foods for the picnic. (L10)
- In the role play area make a picnic environment for children to take their bears on imaginary outings. (L3)

MATHEMATICS

- Talk about the shapes of cakes, biscuits and sandwiches. How many round biscuits are there? (M6)
- Talk about halves as sandwiches are cut. How do we cut it in half fairly? (M6)
- Distribute plates and cups encouraging matching : one for big ted, one for little ted, one for panda etc. (M6).

KNOWLEDGE AND UNDERSTANDING OF THE WORLD

- Make biscuits in the shape of teddies. Discuss the ways materials change as they are cooked. (K8)
- Plan and make food for the picnic. (K8)
- Make place mats for the teddies. How big will they need to be? What pictures would teddies like on their mats? (K8)

PHYSICAL DEVELOPMENT

- Make an obstacle course of large apparatus. Children take teddies along this route to the picnic. (PD2)
- Use fine motor skills in making sandwiches, folding napkins. (PD3)

CREATIVE DEVELOPMENT

- Make accessories for the teddy bears' picnic (See page 20.) (C3, 4)
- Sing 'If you go down to the woods today'. (C3)

ACTIVITY: Planning the picnic

Learning opportunity: As they plan the forthcoming teddy bears' picnic children will discuss the importance of caring for the environment.

Desirable Learning Outcome: Personal and Social Development. Children will learn to treat their environment with care and concern.

Resources: A picture of a picnic scene, a flip-chart.

Organisation: Whole group seated on the floor with flip-chart and picnic scene in clear view.

Key vocabulary: Picnic, litter, clearing up, tidy, untidy.

WHAT TO DO:

Remind the children about the teddy bears' picnic. Look at the picture. What is a picnic? Have they been on any? What do you take on a picnic? Do you bring the same things home? What would happen to anything left behind? How will this change the place visited? Talk about the effects of litter. How can litter be dangerous to other people or wildlife?

Encourage the children to listen carefully to each other and take turns when speaking. As the children talk try to record their ideas on the flip chart in words and pictures. Talk about clearing up tasks and rubbish collecting.

Ask the children to volunteer for different jobs and write their names on a rota. Discuss how jobs are easier and fun when there are other people to work with. Talk about responsibility and how children will need to remember what they promised to do. Display the jobs rota in a prominent place so that children can tick the jobs as they are completed. Divide into groups and begin to prepare for the picnic.

ACTIVITY: Picnic bags

Learning opportunity: Children will develop the skills of cutting, joining and folding as they make a bag.

Desirable Learning Outcome: Creative Development: They explore and select materials and equipment and use skills such as cutting, joining, folding and building for a variety of purposes.

Resources: Paper bags from shops, large sheets of paper, sticky tape or glue, bright felt pens, decorative items such as sequins, glitter, gummed shapes.

Organisation: Small group.

Key vocabulary: Fold, half, join, decorate.

WHAT TO DO:

Explain to the children they will need small bags to carry their food to the picnic. Show them some bags from a variety of shops. Help them to look carefully at how they are made. Point out where the paper is joined or folded.

Explain that the bag needs to be big enough to hold things and strong enough not to break. Show the children how to fold a large oblong of paper in half and to glue or tape along the sides.

Talk about decorations. Some may have shop names or be made from attractive paper. How do they want to decorate theirs? Encourage them to be adventurous.

DISPLAY

Lay a picnic table with a check cloth, plastic party cups and paper plates. Seat the teddies around this. Encourage the children to add party hats, paper napkins, salt dough food and place mats. The food bags and picture menus made by the children could be added to this display.

BRINGING IT ALL TOGETHER

INTRODUCING THE TEDDY BEARS' PICNIC

Explain to the children that in a few days time you are going to hold a teddy bears' picnic. This is something that everyone is going to help to organise and prepare. It will be a lot of hard work!

Talk to the children about picnics. What makes a successful picnic?

Decide on the most convenient time of day to hold the picnic. Discuss this as you encourage the children to talk about the sorts of food which they think would be suitable.

If the picnic is going to be enjoyable what other forms of entertainment might be needed?

Who is going to be invited? If possible, invite other friends and helpers.

Once all the ideas have been noted, plan the sessions leading up to the picnic to allow time for making the most of the preparations. It will not always be possible to hold the picnic out-of-doors, but with a bit of imagination and a few paper flowers dotted around, an indoor venue can become the most luscious of meadows!

MAKING PREPARATIONS

The introductory discussion will have helped children to understand that there are plenty of jobs to be done.

FOOD

Involve the children in deciding what food to prepare. Encourage the children to take decisions about the choice of sandwich fillings, types of biscuit and so on. Some simple market research might be in order! Discuss quantities required. How many bottles of drink do the children think they might need. On the day of the picnic allow all the children to help in the preparation of food. This offers a really useful opportunity to discuss aspects of food hygiene, such as the importance of washing hands. Where is the food going to be kept until it is needed? How should it be wrapped or covered?

INVITATIONS

Encourage the children to think about the sort of information which an invitation needs to give. One approach to this is for you to collect children's ideas and to photocopy an appropriate page. This can then be pasted to the inside of cards which the children design and make.

ACCESSORIES

Talk to the children about all the other things which are needed at a picnic or party. What are they going to use to put the food on? Will decorated napkins be needed, bags to carry food in, party hats or name labels? If so, encourage the children to take responsibility for making them. Remind the children of the teddy bear theme of the picnic as they design their accessories.

PARTY GAMES

Ask the children to think about entertainment at the picnic. Again, you could help some of the older or more able children to carry out a survey to discover the most popular games amongst children in the group. Encourage them to think about a variety of activities, including musical games, ring games, songs and stories.

Here are a few ideas.

GAMES:

- Children march to music carrying teddies. When the music stops, children and teddies 'work' together to make interesting statues.
- Sing 'Here we go down to the Picnic Place' to the tune of 'The Mulberry Bush', substituting actions such as 'This is the way we lay the cloth', ' cut the cake', 'drink some juice'.

SONGS:

- Going on a Bear Hunt
- The Teddy Bear's Picnic
- Me and my Teddy Bear

STORIES:

- Down in the Woods - Nicola Smee
- Old Bear stories - Jane Hissey
- Dr Seuss Bear Stories
- Goldilocks and the Three Bears

RESOURCES

RESOURCES TO COLLECT :

- A variety of toys especially puppets, old and unusual toys.
- Sets of stacking toys such as barrels, pots or Russian dolls.
- Pictures and photographs showing toys and children using toys eg Bruegel's famous painting *Children's Games.*
- A selection of stories about toys.
- Reference books about toys and childhood customs from other countries.
- A few shopping catalogues, preferably with several 'toy' pages.

EVERYDAY RESOURCES:

- Boxes, large and small for modelling.
- Papers and cards of different weights, colours and textures available eg sugar, corrugated card, silver and shiny papers.
- Dry powder paints for mixing and mixed paints for covering large areas such as a model bus.
- Different sized paint brushes from household brushes to thin brushes for delicate work and a variety of paint mixing containers.
- A variety of drawing and colouring pencils, crayons, pastels, charcoals, etc.
- A box of socks, paper bags, paper plates and wooden spoons with wools, raffia, string and other materials for puppet making.
- Additional decorative and finishing materials such as sequins, foils, glitter, tinsel, shiny wools and threads, beads, pieces of textiles, parcel ribbon.

STORIES ABOUT TEDDY BEARS

Bear and Threadbear by Mick Inkpen (Hodder).

The Old Bear series by Jane Hissey (Red Fox).

The Walker Book of Bear Stories - an anthology of well-known titles (Walker).

Where's my Teddy? and *It's the Bear!* by Jez Alborough (Walker).

Teddy Bears series by Susanna Gretz (Puffin).

Winnie the Pooh by AA Milne (Methuen).

STORIES ABOUT OTHER TOYS

The Blue Balloon by Mick Inkpen (Hodder).

Miss Brick the Builder's Baby by Allan Ahlberg and Colin McNaughton (Puffin).

Dogger by Shirley Hughes (Red Fox).

Oi! Get off our Train by John Burningham (Red Fox).

POEMS

This Little Puffin by Elizabeth Matterson (Puffin).

NON-FICTION

What's Inside Toys? (Dorling Kindersley).

Toys in the *My Book About* series (Wayland).

INFORMATION FOR ADULTS

My Puppet Book by Lyn Orton (Salamander Books).

The Know-How Book of Puppets by V Philpott and MJ McNeil (Usbourne).

COLLECTING EVIDENCE OF CHILDREN'S LEARNING

Monitoring children's development is an important task. Keeping a record of children's achievements will help you to see progress and will draw attention to those who are having difficulties. If a child needs additional professional help, such as speech therapy, your records will provide valuable evidence.

Records should be the result of collaboration between group leaders, parents and carers. Parents should be made aware of your record keeping policies when their child joins your group. Show them the type of records you are keeping and make sure they understand that they have an opportunity to contribute. As a general rule, your records should form an open document. Any parent should have access to records relating to his or her child. If you have formal discussions regarding children about whom you have concerns, a dated record of the main points should be kept.

KEEPING IT MANAGEABLE

Records should be helpful in informing group leaders, adult helpers and parents and always be for the benefit of the child. The golden rule is to keep them simple. Make decisions about the sorts of achievements or events which you are going to record. Identifying a clear learning opportunity for each activity will help you to make appropriate judgements about children's capabilities and to record them systematically. Do not attempt to make records following every activity! You can either jot down your observations as they happen or spend some time reflecting on a particular child after a week or so. Aim to complete one sheet per term for each child.

To build up a rounded picture of what each child knows and understands you will need to collect information in a variety of ways such as:

- asking children about their activities and listening to their responses;
- listening to children talking to each other;
- observing children's work such as early writing, drawings, paintings and 3D models;
- making photocopies and photographs of work, video recordings.

INFORMING YOUR PLANNING

Make sure there is a purpose for all this evidence collecting - use it to inform your planning. The column in the sample sheet 'What to aim for next' will help to clarify this. You could also include a 'Plans' column to remind you what to actually do and an 'Evaluation/outcomes' column to highlight progress shown.

Play plan for:______________ Date of birth:______________ Date started:__________ Date finished:__________

Areas of learning	Achievements	What to aim for next:	Parent's/child's views	Plans	Evaluation/outcomes
Personal and Social Development	Being fair with some children. Accepting help and advice.	Continued development of awareness of feelings of others.	Extremely caring of new baby brother at home.	Some pair work, appropriate praise.	16.5 97 Excellent co-operation creating 'road' with David.
Language and Literacy	Reporting. Made up story. Interest in forming names.	Greater interest in books. Ability to establish story from pictures.	Mum - Leo enjoying rhyming at home.	Establish which books interest him and look at and discuss them with him.	23.6.97 Chose lengthy book, interacted, concentrated, showed pleasure.
Mathematics	Number recognition of 1, 2, 3, 4.	Recognition of numbers up to 10. Count up to 10 with ease		More work with 'Galt' number and wooden shapes. Develop estimating.	26.6.97 Enjoying counting. 3. 3.7. 97 Shows addition skills. 10. 7.97 Counts to 10 with ease. Recognises numbers 1-5
Knowledge and Understanding of the World	Understand differences in baby and himself.	Observing differences and odd one out activities. Using colour to develop colour recognition and interest.	Mum slightly concerned about red/green recognition.	Spot the difference activity using colour.	26.6.97 Named R. B. G. Y. with ease. 30.6.97. Talked about different language in Spain.
Physical Development	Good fine skills, attempts hopping.	Hopping, greater balance.		Music/movement activity. Use of new beams.	16.5.97 Cut from large pieces of card straight strips and tiny, detailed vehicle. 19.5.97 Made good attempt to hop - confident.
Creative Development	Continued development in all areas.	3-D work.	Enjoys making models at home.	To extend drawings into junk models.	18.5.97 Produced 'home' for hedgehog.

SKILLS OVERVIEW OF SIX WEEK PLAN

Week	Topic focus	Personal and Social	Language and Literacy	Mathematics	Knowledge and Understanding of the World	Physical	Creative
1	Favourite toys	Caring for toys	Describing toys Recognising names	Describing shape	Exploring materials	Developing motor control	Sensory exploration Use of imagination
2	Construction toys	Co-operating Problem-solving	Discussion Recognising names	Ordering	Building	Balancing	Responding to music Working in three dimensions
3	Moving toys	Describing feelings	Positional language	Describing shape and pattern	Exploring movement	Moving with increasing control	Responding to music Cutting and joining
4	Puppets	Sharing ideas Expressing feelings	Asking questions Story telling	Counting Shape recognition	Cutting and joining Naming of body parts	Moving with control Moving with awareness of others	Working in three dimensions Responding to sounds
5	Special toys	Caring for precious things Awareness of other cultures	Interpreting pictures Stories from other cultures	Describing length and distance Ordering Counting	Experiencing materials Discussing features of the world around us	Using apparatus Moving confidently	Exploring shape and colour Using imagination
6	Teddy bears' picnic	Sharing responsibility Developing awareness of personal hygiene	Using picture symbols	Sharing	Selecting and using materials	Using large apparatus	Using materials Enjoying song, dance and games

HOME LINKS

The theme of toys lends itself to useful links with children's homes and families. Through working together children and adults gain respect for each other and build comfortable and confident relationships.

ESTABLISHING PARTNERSHIPS

- Keep parents informed about the topic of Toys, and the themes for each week. By understanding the work of the group, parents will enjoy the involvement of contributing ideas, time and resources.
- Photocopy the parent's page for each child to take home.
- Invite friends, childminders and families to share the teddy bears' picnic.

USING LIVING MEMORY

- Invite adults known to the children to come and talk about the toys they played with as children.
- Invite older friends and relatives to recollect some of the playground games that they played as children. These could be recorded in a book to be shared by everyone.

RESOURCE REQUESTS

- Old toys are often very precious possessions. However, some owners might be willing to bring old 'friends' into the group and to talk about their stories.
- Ask to borrow pictures and photographs which show children at play.

If you are making a display it is better to photocopy these rather than risk damaging them.

PREPARING THE PICNIC

- Depending on the scale of operations, preparing the picnic food may be a case of 'all hands on deck'! Although the children should be as involved as possible, they will clearly need a great deal of support. Any additional help will be of great value.